MRJC
12/14

D1562386

Great Women in History

Wilma Mankiller

by Abby Colich

Content Consultant: Julie L. Reed,
Assistant Professor, American Indian History,
University of Tennessee

Consulting Editor: Gail Saunders-Smith, PhD

CAPSTONE PRESS
a capstone imprint

Pebble Books are published by Capstone Press,
1710 Roe Crest Drive, North Mankato, Minnesota 56003.
www.capstonepub.com

Library of Congress Cataloging-in-Publication Data
Colich, Abby.
Wilma Mankiller / by Abby Colich.
     pages cm.— (Pebble books. Great women in history)
 Includes bibliographical references and index.
 Audience: Grades K–3.
 ISBN 978-1-4914-0540-6 (library binding)
 ISBN 978-1-4914-0543-7 (pbk.)
 ISBN 978-1-4914-0546-8 (ebook PDF)
 1. Mankiller, Wilma Pearl, 1945–2010—Juvenile literature. 2. Cherokee women—
Biography—Juvenile literature. 3. Cherokee Indians—Kings and rulers—
Biography—Juvenile literature. I. Title.
 E99.C5M332 2015
 973.04975570092—dc23
 [B]   2013047242

Photo Credits
Alamy Images/Buddy Mays, cover, 18; AP Images: 14, Dennis Cook, 20, Jerry
Willis, 10; Corbis/Bettmann, 16; John Elk III, 6; Courtesy of the Oklahoma Historical
Society/Chester R. Cowen Collection, 12; San Francisco History Center, San Francisco
Public Library, 8; Shutterstock/Transia Design, cover art; Wikimedia/Caleb Long, 4

Note to Parents and Teachers

The Great Women in History set supports national social studies standards related to
people and culture. This book describes and illustrates Wilma Mankiller. The images
support early readers in understanding the text. The repetition of words and phrases
helps early readers learn new words. This book also introduces early readers to
subject-specific vocabulary words, which are defined in the Glossary section. Early
readers may need assistance to read some words and to use the Table of Contents,
Glossary, Read More, Internet Sites, and Index sections of the book.

Printed in the United States of America in Stevens Point, Wisconsin.
032014   008092WZF14

Table of Contents

1945

born

Early Life

Wilma Mankiller was the first female chief of the Cherokee Nation. She was born in 1945 in Tahlequah, Oklahoma. Wilma had 10 brothers and sisters.

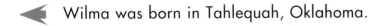
Wilma was born in Tahlequah, Oklahoma.

1945

born

Young Wilma played games and listened to stories about Cherokee people. People in her community helped each other. In the Cherokee language, this is called *gadugi* (gah-DOO-gee).

A lake near Wilma's home

1945
born

1956
moves to
California

Wilma's family was poor.
They had no electricity,
phones, or running water.
In 1956 they moved to
California. The Mankillers
hoped to find a better life.

◀ Wilma's neighborhood in California

1945
born

1956
moves to
California

Young Adult

In California Wilma met other American Indians. They taught her about their cultures. She helped them fight to get the U.S. government to follow its treaties.

1945 born

1956 moves to California

1963 gets married

Wilma married Hector Hugo Olaya de Bardi in 1963. They had two daughters, Felicia and Gina. Wilma later started taking college classes. She and Hugo divorced in 1974.

1945 born

1956 moves to California

1963 gets married

1977 returns to Oklahoma

14

Life's Work

Wilma and her daughters moved back to Oklahoma in 1977. Wilma helped the town of Bell get running water. In 1985 Wilma became the Cherokee Nation's first female chief.

Wilma in 1985

1985

becomes
Cherokee chief

15

1945
born

1956
moves to
California

1963
gets
married

1977
returns to
Oklahoma

As chief, Wilma carried on the tradition of gadugi. She created new health centers, helped people get jobs, and started programs for children. Wilma's work improved Cherokee life.

Wilma at a meeting with President Reagan (left)

1985

becomes Cherokee chief

1945
born

1956
moves to
California

1963
gets
married

1977
returns to
Oklahoma

Later Years

Wilma ended her time as chief in 1995. She still volunteered and worked with Cherokee people. She also wrote books and taught college classes.

Wilma with Cherokee children

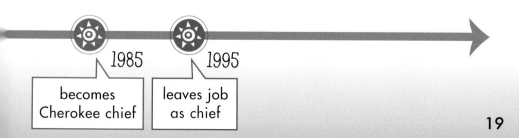

1985
becomes
Cherokee chief

1995
leaves job
as chief

1945 born

1956 moves to California

1963 gets married

1977 returns to Oklahoma

Wilma received many honors for her work. In 1998 she received the Presidential Medal of Freedom. This is one of the country's highest awards. She died in 2010.

◀ Wilma receiving the Presidential Medal of Freedom

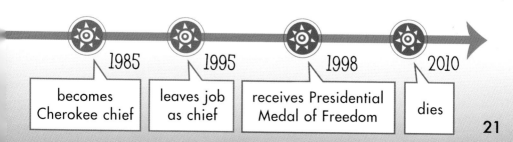

1985 — becomes Cherokee chief

1995 — leaves job as chief

1998 — receives Presidential Medal of Freedom

2010 — dies

Glossary

chief—the leader of a group of people

community—a group of people who live in the same area

culture—a people's way of life, ideas, customs, and traditions

gadugi—the Cherokee word for people working together

government—the group of people who make laws, rules, and decisions for a country or state

nation—a group of people with the same language, customs, and government

tradition—a custom, idea, or belief passed down through time

treaty—a written agreement between countries or groups of people. A treaty is signed by the people's leaders.

volunteer—to offer to do something without pay

Read More

Dorman, Robert L. *Oklahoma: Past and Present.* United States: Past and Present. New York: Rosen Central, 2011.

Kissock, Heather, and Rachel Small. *Cherokee: American Indian Art and Culture.* New York: Weigl Publishers Inc., 2011.

Weil, Ann, and Charlotte Guillain. *American Indian Cultures.* Global Cultures. Chicago: Heinemann Library, 2013.

Internet Sites

FactHound offers a safe, fun way to find Internet sites related to this book. All of the sites on FactHound have been researched by our staff.

Here's all you do:

Visit *www.facthound.com*

Type in this code: 9781491405406

Check out projects, games and lots more at
www.capstonekids.com

Critical Thinking Using the Common Core

1. How did Wilma's childhood and early life prepare her to become chief of the Cherokee Nation? (Key Ideas and Details)

2. Look at the pictures of Wilma. How can you tell that she is proud of her culture? (Craft and Structure)

Index

Word Count: 241
Grade: 1
Early-Intervention Level: 20

Editorial Credits
Nikki Bruno Clapper, editor; Terri Poburka, designer; Kelly Garvin, media researcher; Tori Abraham, production specialist